D0324270

THE·LITTLE BIRTHDAY BOOK

By
Suzanne Beilenson

Design by
SCHARR DESIGN

PETER PAUPER PRESS, INC.
WHITE PLAINS · NEW YORK

CONTENTS

Introduction   3

Birthsigns   5

Birthstones. 21

Quotations 37

Famous Birthdays. 41

Birthday Register 53

For Esther

Copyright © 1990
Peter Pauper Press, Inc.
202 Mamaroneck Avenue
White Plains, NY 10601
ISBN 0-88088-363-4
Library of Congress No. 90-61142
Printed in the United States of America
5   4   3   2   1

INTRODUCTION

Whether you are 8 or 80 (or 3 or 24 or 98), there is only one day a year that you can call your very own—your birthday. Of course, you may share the date with a famous celeb' or two, but that only means a bigger party!

Your birthday determines a whole assortment of facts and figures about you. Every birthday has a zodiacal sign and special gem attached to it, which influence your personality. If, for example, you were born on April 10th, your birthsign is Aries (a fiery and energetic character) and diamonds are indeed your best friend.

Use this Little Birthday Book to fathom just why it is you do what you do. After you fully understand yourself, you might do a little research on your family and friends—and that special love interest!

Everyone hates to have his or her birthday forgotten. So mark them all down in the Birthday Register, and remember to say "Happy Birthday!"

S.B.

Introduction

The zodiac, as conceived by astrologers more than 2,000 years ago, is an imaginary band of stars that appears to encircle the earth. Astrology associates life on earth with the movement of the zodiac.

The band is divided into twelve parts. Each houses a specific constellation which represents a different birthsign. As the earth (or to the early astrologers, the zodiac) rotates throughout the year, each sign "rules" for approximately a month. A person's birthday determines which sign influences his or her life. However, a person may be born on the "cusp," the changeover days between a departing sign and a new ruling sign. In this case, it is necessary to study the traits of both signs to understand one's self.

Each sign also has one "ruling planet" from which it derives its main characteristics. In addition, one of four elements—fire, earth, air and water—is attributed to each sign. The fire signs (Aries, Leo, and Saggitarius) are known for being ardent and keen. The earth signs (Taurus, Virgo and Capricorn) are generally regarded as practical and cautious. Air signs (Gemini, Libra, and Aquarius) tend to be the most articulate and intellectual, while the water signs (Cancer, Scorpio and Pisces) usually are the most emotional of the group.

Furthermore, every birthsign is associated with a particular part of the human body. The zodiac unfolds from head to toe: Aries relates to the head, Taurus to the neck and shoulders, Gemini to the arms and lungs, Cancer to the stomach, Leo to the heart, Virgo to the intestines, Libra to the kidneys and lower back, Scorpio to the reproductive organs, Sagittarius to the thighs, Capricorn to the knees, Aquarius to the calves and ankles, and Pisces to the feet. A person's corresponding body part can be the source of his or her greatest strength, but may also be the locale of injury or distress.

Aries, the Ram
March 21 to April 19

As the first sign of the zodiac, Aries contains all the characteristics of the newborn. The Ram is innocent, ignorant, and commands everyone else's full attention. Similarly, the Ram does not ask for love, but rather demands it. Behind the proud front, though, lurks an insecure Aries who fears a mate's desertion. One must constantly reassure this babe of the zodiac of one's undying affection.

Ruled by Mars, Aries takes on many of the qualities of the Roman war god for which the planet is named. A true leader, an Aries can count on being bold, confident, and enthusiastic. A lover of speed, the Ram walks fast and drives faster. Aries' impulsive nature can lead to recklessness, but if this trait is harnessed, Aries will be revealed as a truly adventurous and pioneering spirit.

Aries make great entrepreneurs because they are impervious to risk and bounce back quickly from defeat. It is safe to invest in an Aries venture. The Ram is careful with other people's money, though the Aries may spend all of his or her cash at the first sign of a "sale."

Aries also do well in careers such as advertising, the military, public service, hair dressing, and television production.

Taurus, the Bull
April 20 to May 20

Taurus emulates many characteristics of the Bull for whom he is named. Often stubborn, Taurus has loads of patience and determination. The Bull may be slow to anger, but when finally provoked, makes a terrifying adversary.

Venus, the planet named for the goddess of love, rules Taurus, inspiring a love of beauty, music, and art in the Bull. Taurus also has a wonderful sense of humor and is generally amiable and physically affectionate. The Bull views love as an uncomplicated and happy venture. Taurus makes a good spouse, for the Bull is faithful, reliable, and always pays the bills on time.

Known as the "money sign," Taurus worships the dollar—not for itself, but simply for the ease and pleasure which it brings. Financial affairs are handled in an orderly and efficient manner. The Bull is happy to loan a friend money, but will always charge interest. With such qualities, the Bull makes a good banker or businessperson. Other bully careers include real estate, insurance, and architecture, as well as certain careers in the arts.

Gemini, the Twins
May 21 to June 21

Like the Twins who represent Gemini, this birthsign often seems to have the energy of two. Geminis are quick, agile and bounding with nervous energy. Never boring, they adore romance and the chase involved. Yet they do not rely on love's security and are therefore apt to fly away at the drop of a hat.

The intellectual Geminis love conversation and witty repartee, and they can easily argue both sides of an issue. No wonder the Twins are ruled by Mercury, the planet named for the god of communication! Geminis also draw on Mercury's characteristics of versatility, adaptability and speed. Understandably, the Twins excel in sales, journalism, radio, and any job related to transportation.

However, with so much energy and so many interests, Geminis often overextend themselves. If the fickle Twins are not careful, they will find their attics filled with uncompleted projects that got lost in the shuffle.

Cancer, the Crab
June 22 to July 22

To a certain extent, Cancerians reflect the traits of the symbol, the Crab. They have a hard, protective shell which makes them difficult to get to know. Underneath, however, Cancerians are kind, sympathetic, and the most vulnerable of all the birthsigns.

The Moon, which rules over the emotional Cancers, confers upon them its qualities of imagination, intuitiveness, and sometimes moodiness. The Moon also symbolizes the feminine principle, perhaps explaining Cancer's nurturing aspect. Cancers equate love with emotional security, and so their mates must continually reassure this fearful birthsign of their affection.

Crabs are often interested in the occult and other types of mysticism. It is also not unusual to find a Cancer sitting by a window daydreaming. Occasionally this dreaminess causes Crabs to be unrealistic in terms of money and to live far beyond their means.

Though they may part with their money quickly, Crabs are successful creatures in their chosen professions.

Cancers shine in any field which helps others: They make wonderful doctors, nurses, zoologists, and teachers.

Leo, the Lion
July 23 to August 22

Of all the birthsigns, Leo most resembles its animal counterpart. Like the Lion, a Leo commands authority, demands respect, and roars when dissatisfied. However, Leo is a benevolent ruler, treating his or her circle of friends with a returned respect and great kindness. A Leo's mate will be showered with affection and romance as this birthsign loves to love.

The extroverted Lion owes its cheerful disposition and generosity to the Sun, which governs the birthsign. The Sun also bestows Leos with vitality, passion, and ambition. The drive to succeed and a fear of failure often turn Leos into workaholics and exacting bosses. The Lion also has a flair for the dramatic, which is often misinterpreted as arrogance and egotism.

Still, the Lion loves the limelight, and consequently makes much of appearances. Leos find satisfaction as actors, singers, models, chefs, and politicians.

Virgo, the Virgin
August 23 to September 22

Reflecting the Virgin's attractive traits of youth, beauty, and purity, Virgos rarely look their true age. However, Virgos are quite modest and more interested in helping others than themselves. Similarly, in the affairs of the heart, a Virgo's mate will find this birthsign to be gently devoted and attentive.

Virgos possess a keen intelligence and a great enjoyment of learning, which they owe partially to the influence of Mercury, named for the god of communication. The logical Virgos also have exceptional powers of observation, which makes them very good journalists, critics, and doctors.

Virgos pay an enormous amount of attention to detail (almost to a fault), and are perfectionists about everything. These qualities, combined with the Virgo's fondness of solitude, makes this birthsign a natural as an accountant, statistician, or librarian.

Libra, the Scales
September 23 to October 23

The Scales represent balance, harmony, and justice, making Libras natural peacemakers. Libras are agreeable, steady, tolerant, and are known throughout the zodiac as the diplomats of the heavens.

Venus's influence enhances the just nature of the Libra with a love of beauty and gentleness. This cultured, artistic side of the birthsign only adds to the Libra's diplomatic powers. Thanks to Venus, Libras make fine painters, writers, and designers, in addition to politicians, diplomats, and judges.

However, the ability to see both sides of an issue can cause indecision in Libras, and they often find it difficult to say no because of their overwhelming desire to please. Yet this quality is beneficial when it comes to personal relationships.

Although not the most spontaneous sign, the Libra's talent for getting along with everyone makes him or her a popular socialite and a desirable spouse.

Scorpio, the Scorpion
October 24 to November 21

Like their symbol, Scorpios are apt to sting themselves rather than let anyone else hurt them first. Yet once the insecure Scorpion's trust is won (and it must be won), the Scorpion will willingly sacrifice himself or herself for a loved one.

The courage and intensity of this loyalty stems from Scorpio's ruling planet Mars, named for the Roman god of war. With strength, however, also comes a quick temper, a sarcastic tongue, and a secretive personality—the armor behind which the Scorpio hides his fear of not being liked, or worse, being betrayed. Consequently, Scorpios work best alone, often as detectives, doctors, and chefs, although a career in the military also suits this aggressive birthsign.

In their personal lives, Scorpios yearn for love in spite of their suspiciousness of others. Once this is overcome, their mates will be amply rewarded in the bedroom for their perseverance and understanding. The power of Mars generates enormous passion and sensitivity.

Sagittarius, the Archer or Centaur
November 22 to December 21

Bow and arrow in hand, the Archer confidently gallops around in search of fun, freedom, and adventure. Indeed, a Sagittarius dares not only to dream but also to pursue his or her goals, sometimes to the point of recklessness.

Luckily, Jupiter rules over this birthsign, endowing Sagittarius with strength, health, and good fortune. Also possessed by an unending curiosity, the cheerful Archer wanders the world searching for answers to life's mysteries. However, this search eventually turns inward as the Archer seeks truth within himself or herself. Sagittarians therefore make excellent philosophers and lawyers while also proving successful in the fields of travel, theater, and exploration.

The need for adventure combined with an irresponsible attitude toward money can take a toll on the Archer's family. Sagittarians need an equally independent and daring mate, but one who can take care of the loose ends left in their wake.

Capricorn, the Goat
December 22 to January 19

The sure-footed Goat easily climbs the mountain of success in all that he or she endeavors. Challenges are met with aplomb, obstacles are overcome with determination, and goals are always kept in sight.

Capricorns can thank their ruling planet Saturn for the discipline and self-control which drive them to achieve. Saturn, named for the Roman god of the harvest and planting, also endows Capricorns with a strong sense of family and tradition. With a dependable Capricorn in the family, there will always be money in the bank and a turkey on Thanksgiving.

Having such steady values and ambition, Goats do well in most careers, although their business acumen lends itself to banking, accounting, and real estate. The seriousness of these professions, however, tends to belie the humorous and fun side of the Goat.

Still, a Goat's mate should not expect displays of emotion or excessive sentimentality (the conservative Goat just hates a scene!), but one can count on this birthsign for a loyal and enduring love to last a lifetime.

Aquarius, the Water Carrier
January 20 to February 18

The Water Carrier is never depicted simply bearing the Cup of Life, but rather pouring its contents forth. Similarly, Aquarians pour their knowledge and idealism into the world around them in the hope of achieving a better society. Aquarians are the true humanitarians of the zodiac, believing in equality, generosity, and the brotherhood of man.

If the Aquarian ideal seems a bit unrealistic, blame it on the sign's ruling planet Uranus, named for the Greek god of the heavens. Aquarian heads may be in the clouds, but this only makes them creative, inventive, and capable of abstract thought. Successful Aquarians may be found in fields relating to politics and social work, as well as the arts, advertising, and the sciences.

On a personal level, Aquarians have a great respect for other people (even if they do not particularly esteem figures of authority). However they do not form many close friendships, perhaps because the Aquarian outlook differs so much from most others. Yet an unselfish attitude toward love and deep-seated loyalty make an Aquarian a great addition to any family.

Pisces, the Fishes
February 19 to March 20

The Pisces' symbol of two fish swimming in opposite directions accurately reflects this birthsign's difficulty in choosing a definitive course in life. Every person and every situation makes an impression on Pisces, and it is this ultrasensitivity which causes Pisces' confusion.

However, Neptune's watery influence on Pisces turns sensitivity into adaptability. Pisces easily "drifts with the tide," enjoying a vast array of life's experiences ranging from the psychic to the romantic. And when it comes to romance, gentle Pisces is an artist. However, the slippery Fish will often do just about anything to escape love's hooks. (One shouldn't even *think* the word "commitment" around this birthsign or chance Pisces swimming into other waters!)

A lost mate, however, can usually find his or her Pisces counterpart near the water. Pisces makes a great deep-sea diver, plumber, ski instructor, physical therapist, or even waterbed salesperson. If Pisces still remains missing, one should remember the Fish's philosophical and creative bent. Oftentimes, Pisces devotes his or herself to religion, writing, or teaching.

Ideal Astrological Love Matches

Aries—*Leo*

Aries—*Sagittarius*

Taurus—*Virgo*

Taurus—*Capricorn*

Cancer—*Scorpio*

Cancer—*Pisces*

Leo—*Sagittarius*

Virgo—*Capricorn*

Libra—*Gemini*

Libra—*Aquarius*

Scorpio—*Pisces*

Aquarius—*Gemini*

BIRTHSTONES

Introduction

Gemstones have held a special significance since Biblical times. The original breastplate of the High Priest of the Hebrews contained 12 precious gems, representing the 12 tribes of Israel (see Exodus 39:10-14). And, according to Revelations, the foundations of the walls of the heavenly New Jerusalem are garnished with 12 gemstones (Revelations 21: 12-21).

Throughout history, each precious or semi-precious birthstone was associated with different beliefs or superstitions. The ancient Greeks and Romans often linked a birthstone with a god and his or her dominant qualities. In the Middle Ages, stones were thought to possess curative powers. Stones would be placed on the body part in pain, or were ground into powder and swallowed. Today, astrologers simply believe that a birthstone suggests several basic characteristics of an individual's zodiacal sign.

Long before the Roman calendar came into usage, a gem was assigned to each sign of the zodiac. It was not until the 16th Century, however, that gemstones became linked to a specific month of the year. (You can choose either method to determine what your birthstone is!) In addition, some months and zodiac signs also have alternative birthstones from which to choose.

Garnet
Capricorn and January

Garnets possess a luminescent quality, and for this reason some believe that they were the only light source on Noah's Ark. Most commonly, garnets are red, but they are found in a variety of colors.

Constancy and fidelity are attributed to the garnet. The stone is thought to promote the popularity and financial success of its wearer, but also to guard against bad dreams and depression. The Crusaders, on their travels to the Holy Land, wore garnets to ward off accidents and to protect them from wounds.

Red garnets were once used to reduce fever, while yellow garnets were employed to cure jaundice.

Amethyst
Aquarius and February

This purple quartz derives its name from the Greek word *amethystos,* meaning "without drunkenness." According to legend, the goddess Diana turned the lovely Greek maiden Amethyst into sparkling white stone in vengeance against the god Bacchus. Bacchus, remorseful at the innocent girl's fate, poured grape wine over her stone figure, transforming it into the brilliant violet color known today as amethyst.

The amethyst has traditionally signified power, especially to royalty; from this tradition comes the phrase "royal purple." Cleopatra favored this jewel. In the Roman Catholic church, the Pope wears an amethyst ring known as the Bishop's Stone. St. Valentine also claims the amethyst as his stone, and for this reason lovers will find that it smooths their bumpy paths.

An amethyst sharpens the wits and gives victory in battle. It prevents sleepiness and violent passions, while it guards its wearer from the powers of sorcery.

Bloodstone
Pisces and March

Bloodstone's graphic name comes from an association with the crucifixion of Jesus Christ. It was said that some drops of his blood fell onto the green jasper stones at his feet, creating a new green gem sprinkled with red particles.

Understandably, this bi-colored stone (also known as **Heliotrope**) stops bleeding, especially nose bleeds, but it also helps cure tumors and draw the poison out of snakes. During the Renaissance, people believed that a bloodstone could make the wearer invisible. Bloodstone is also associated with bravery, steadfast affection, wisdom, and the powers of deduction.

Bloodstone's alternative is the **Aquamarine**, a transparent blue-green stone. The ancient Greeks called it the Stone of Neptune, the god of the sea. The aquamarine is also known as the sailor's stone, because it assures safe voyages.

Diamond
Aries and April

The word "diamond" is derived from the Latin and Greek word *adamas*, meaning invincible, a definition most certainly suited to this hardest of all minerals. Although the most popular diamonds are colorless and transparent, this gem comes in a variety of colors, even in red.

In the Middle Ages, many believed that diamonds protected the wearer against sorcery and plague, and promoted heroism. Use a diamond as an antidote for poison (in the relationship?), to stop delirium, or simply to ease worry.

The gem can also test a lover's fidelity. If placed on a sleeping lover's brow without the lover's knowledge, the faithful mate will turn towards his or her beloved, while the unfaithful will roll away.

The diamond makes an excellent engagement ring. Diamond helps the wearer to resist temptation, and signifies purity, innocence, and (if need be) repentance!

Emerald
Taurus and May

The emerald takes its name from the Persian word *zummurrud*, meaning green. The ancient Persians believed that emeralds ensured security and peace of mind, and that they had medicinal value for liver, stomach, and eye ailments.

The Roman emperor Nero was said to have possessed a large emerald that he used as an eyeglass. Scholars today suspect that it was actually an aquamarine which, like the emerald, comes from the mineral beryl but is more transparent.

Emeralds were introduced to Western Europe in the Middle Ages and became very popular. Henry II of England received an emerald ring when in 1171 he was crowned King of Ireland. Ireland became known as the "Emerald Isle" because of that historical fact, and because of its lush, green countryside.

Emeralds symbolize loyalty, friendship, and contentment. They are thought to bestow the gift of prophecy (or perhaps of blarney) on the wearer, detect poisons in the body, and even protect the chastity of women.

Pearl
Gemini and June

The Arabians believed that pearls were formed by drops of rain falling into open oyster shells, and called these gems "the tears of the gods." Pearls were greatly sought after by the ancient Arabians and Persians both for their decorative beauty and for their supposed power to cure insanity.

Cleopatra, to demonstrate her wealth and power to an attending Mark Anthony, was said to have dissolved a pearl in vinegar and then to have drunk the mixture! The pearl is associated with Cleopatra, so it is not surprising that it symbolizes youth and beauty. The pearl, however, also represents purity, innocence, and good health.

June's alternative birthstone is the **Moonstone**. This opalescent translucent gem comes in a variety of tints, but is best known as colorless. Moonstone's name derives from the belief that the Roman moon goddess Diana was trapped inside the gem.

The stone's power is thought to vary according to the movements of the moon. As the moon waxes, moonstone works as a love charm; as the moon wanes, the gem bestows the gift of prophecy.

Ruby
Cancer and July

This rarest of all the birthstones has traditionally signified wealth and riches. The finest rubies have always been mined in Myanmar (formerly Burma), and the Burmese ruler was centuries ago known as the "King of the Rubies."

The luminescent quality of the ruby led the ancient Asians to deem it the "glowing stone." Its modern name is derived from the Latin word *ruber* meaning red. The Romans identified the ruby with Mars, the god of war, and so the stone came to represent his attributes of nobility, aggressiveness, and courage.

King Henry V of England wore an exceptional ruby in 1415 during the pivotal battle against the French at Agincourt. Armed with the powers of Mars, he and his forces carried the day in a stunning upset.

Sardonyx
Leo and August

Sardonyx, which occurs in alternating layers of reddish sand and onyx, derives its name from the Greek word *sard* meaning reddish brown and the Latin word *onyx* meaning veiled gem.

This birthstone is most often used in the production of cameos. A white figure is cut from the upper layer, exposing the lower reddish brown layer as background.

Roman warriors wore cameos bearing the likenesses of Mars or Hercules to bring them bravery in battle. The sardonyx was also believed to relieve eye pain, to guard against infection, and to act as an antidote to the poisonous bites of insects and snakes.

The stone brings (a perhaps sardonic) eloquence to its wearer, and symbolizes marital happiness.

The alternative August birthstone is the **Peridot**. This green, transparent gem is found mainly on a small island in the Red Sea, but has also been discovered in anthills of the American Southwest and in meteorites. The peridot protects its wearer against sadness, fear, and enchantment.

Sapphire
Virgo and September

Sapphire is named for the Greek island of Sappherine in the Arabian Sea where this stone was found in ancient times. While the word sapphire connotes a blue stone, sapphires actually range through the spectrum of colors. The largest blue sapphire was unearthed in Burma in 1929. Known as the "Gem of the Jungle," this sapphire weighed 958 carats and was later cut into nine extremely valuable large stones.

The ancient Greeks assigned the sapphire to Apollo, the god of prophecy, and thus the gem was thought to have prophetic qualities. Sapphires were also prized for their great medicinal assets. It is said that they cured hysteria, fever, and boils, and protected against pestilence, snake bites, and eye diseases.

Sapphires are regarded as the most spiritual of all the birthstones. They are known as priestly gems, symbolic of the sky and heavens. Sapphires also signify truth and sincerity.

Opal
Libra and October

This unusual birthstone derives its name from the Sanskrit word for jewel. The most popular variety of the opal is milky white and opaque, but the gem shimmers with colors as light is refracted in its many layers.

The opal has historically enjoyed a flawed reputation, in spite of its supposed power to strengthen the heart, prevent fainting and infection, and guard against inconstancy. Opal acquired a reputation for bad luck during the Black Death plague which ravaged Europe during the 14th Century. The stone appeared brilliant until the moment of the patient's death, and then suddenly darkened; people therefore believed that the opal had caused the death. Today, doctors attribute the gem's lost luster to the change in the wearer's body temperature.

The superstitious need not worry, however, for there is an alternative birthstone to the opal. The **Tourmaline**, dubbed the rainbow stone because of its wide range of color, dispels fear and promotes success. It possesses remarkable electrical properties; when rubbed, it becomes charged and behaves like a magnet. Benjamin Franklin used tourmalines in his early studies of electricity.

Topaz
Scorpio and November

The topaz takes its name from the Sanskrit word for fire, and indeed, the best-known variety of the topaz is a fiery yellow. However, this transparent gem comes in other colors—though the golden topaz is still the most popular and quite rare.

It was once believed that the topaz derived its powers from the sun, perhaps because of its luminescent quality. Hence, the gem signifies strength, cheerfulness, and friendship.

In medieval times, people believed that one could cool boiling water instantly by dropping a topaz into it, and that a woman could lessen the pains of childbirth by holding a topaz in her hand. The gem was thought to protect the wearer against enchantment and sorcery. On a more daily basis, the topaz would stimulate the appetite, ensure sound sleep, and prevent asthma.

Turquoise
Sagittarius and December

Turquoise ranges in color from blue to green, but the most sought-after turquoise is sky-blue.

The turquoise, named for the Turkish merchants who brought it to Europe, is the earliest-known gemstone. Archeologists searching through an Egyptian tomb in 1900 found four fabulous turquoise bracelets on the mummified arm of Queen Zer, who ruled in 5500 B.C. Interestingly, the American Indians of the Southwest consider the turquoise to be the guardian of tombs, and it is the only gem allowed in their graves.

The turquoise has been used as an antidote for scorpion stings, as protection against the evil eye and from falling, and as a love charm. The stone should bring to its wearer prosperity, good fortune, and success.

Sagittarians may also adopt **Zircon**, usually a colorless gem, as their birthstone. Zircon is thought to work against evil influences, plagues, and poisons. It can also increase the wearer's wealth, wisdom, and honor.

Birthstones in Rhyme

Let JANUARY's maiden be
All GARNET gemmed with CONSTANCY.

In fitful FEBRUARY it's a verity
The AMETHYST denotes SINCERITY.

But oh, what shall a MARCH maid do?
Wear a BLOODSTONE and be FIRM and TRUE.

The APRIL girl has a brave defense
The DIAMOND guards her INNOCENCE.

Sweet child of MAY you'll taste the caress
Of EMERALD's promised HAPPINESS.

PEARLS for JUNE girls the precious wealth,
And to crown it all they bring her HEALTH.

The RUBY stole a spark from heav'n above,
To bring the JULY maiden fervent LOVE,

The AUGUST maiden with sweet simplicity
Wears SARDONYX, gem of FELICITY.

Out of the depths shall SAPPHIRES come
Bringing SEPTEMBER's child WISDOM.

OCTOBER's child in darkness oft may grope,
The iridescent OPAL bids it HOPE.

Born in NOVEMBER happy is she,
Whom the TOPAZ teaches FIDELITY.

DECEMBER's child shall live to bless
The TURQUOISE that insures SUCCESS.

Birthstones Through the Week

Ancient astrologers have designated birthstones corresponding to the days of the week, as follows:

Sunday	*Pearl*
Monday	*Emerald*
Tuesday	*Topaz*
Wednesday	*Turquoise*
Thursday	*Sapphire*
Friday	*Ruby*
Saturday	*Amethyst*

If you desire variety in the gems that you wear, try these alternatives—and see who else is wearing them!

QUOTATIONS

Monday's child is fair of face,
Tuesday's child is full of grace,
Wednesday's child is full of woe,
Thursday's child has far to go,
Friday's child is loving and giving,
Saturday's child works hard for its living,
And a child that's born on the Sabbath day
Is fair and wise and good and gay.

UNKNOWN

The man who views the world at 50 the same as he did at 20 has wasted 30 years of his life.

MUHAMMAD ALI

Women are most fascinating between the ages of 35 and 40 after they have won a few races and know how to pace themselves. Since few women ever pass 40, maximum fascination can continue indefinitely.

CHRISTIAN DIOR

To exclude from position of trust and command all those below the age of 44 would have kept Jefferson from writing the Declaration of Independence, Washington from commanding the Continental Army, Madison from fathering the Constitution, Hamilton from serving as Secretary of the Treasury, Clay from being elected Speaker of the House, and Christopher Columbus from even discovering America.

JOHN F. KENNEDY

I find I am always glad when the birthday is over. Then you have another whole year. The most difficult ones are the ones that end with a zero—20, 30, 40, 50, 60, whatever. Those are the hard ones. The others are sort of rest periods between the zeros.

ROBERT J. DOLE,
on his 62nd birthday

I'm very pleased with each advancing year. It stems back to when I was forty. I was a bit upset about reaching that milestone, but an older friend consoled me. "Don't complain about growing old—many people don't have that privilege."

EARL WARREN

38

Yes, I'm 68, but when I was a boy I was too poor to smoke, so knock off ten years. That makes me 58. And since I never developed the drinking habit, you can knock off ten more years. So I'm 48—in the prime of my life. Retire? Retire to what?

W. A. C. BENNETT

When you hit seventy, you eat better, you sleep sounder, you feel more alive than when you were thirty. Obviously, it's healthier to have women on your mind than on your knees.

MAURICE CHEVALIER

When I was 14, I was the oldest I ever was. . . .I've been getting younger ever since.

SHIRLEY TEMPLE

Retire? That's ridiculous. What does it for you is to have something to get up for in the morning. Now, they say, you should retire at 70. When I was 70, I still had pimples.

GEORGE BURNS

How old would you be if you didn't know how old you was?

SATCHEL PAIGE

FAMOUS BIRTHDAYS
Who else was born on your birthday?

January

1	1735	Paul Revere
1	1895	J. Edgar Hoover
3	1793	Lucretia Mott
4	1914	Jane Wyman
4	1937	Dyan Cannon
6	1412	Joan of Arc
6	1913	Loretta Young
6	1914	Danny Thomas
7	1800	Millard Fillmore
8	1912	Jose Ferrer
8	1947	David Bowie
9	1904	George Balanchine
9	1913	Richard M. Nixon
9	1914	Gypsy Rose Lee
9	1941	Joan Baez
11	1842	William James
11	1930	Rod Taylor
12	1856	John Singer Sargent
12	1876	Jack London
14	1741	Benedict Arnold
14	1941	Faye Dunaway
15	1913	Lloyd Bridges
15	1929	Martin Luther King, Jr.
16	1909	Ethel Merman
17	1706	Benjamin Franklin
17	1860	Anton Chekhov
17	1931	James Earl Jones
18	1782	Daniel Webster
18	1882	A. A. Milne
18	1904	Cary Grant
18	1913	Danny Kaye
18	1942	Muhammad Ali

19	1807	Robert E. Lee
19	1809	Edgar Allen Poe
19	1839	Paul Cezanne
19	1946	Dolly Parton
20	1896	George Burns
20	1920	Federico Fellini
20	1937	Joan Rivers
21	1824	Stonewall Jackson
21	1942	Mac Davis
22	1561	Francis Bacon
22	1849	Johan August Strindberg
23	1783	Stendhal
23	1933	Chita Rivera
24	1862	Edith Wharton
24	1917	Ernest Borgnine
25	1759	Robert Burns
25	1874	W. Somerset Maugham
26	1880	Douglas MacArthur
26	1928	Eartha Kitt
27	1756	Mozart
27	1832	Lewis Carroll
27	1885	Jerome Kern
27	1921	Donna Reed
28	1886	Artur Rubinstein
28	1948	Mikhail Baryshnikov
29	1737	Thomas Paine
29	1843	William McKinley
29	1880	W. C. Fields
29	1939	Germaine Greer
30	1882	Franklin D. Roosevelt
30	1931	Gene Hackman
31	1797	Franz Schubert
31	1903	Tallulah Bankhead
31	1923	Norman Mailer

February

1	1895	John Ford
1	1901	Clark Gable
2	1901	Jascha Heifetz
3	1809	Felix Mendelssohn
3	1874	Gertrude Stein
3	1894	Norman Rockwell
4	1902	Charles A. Lindbergh
4	1921	Betty Friedan
5	1919	Red Buttons
6	1756	Aaron Burr
6	1895	Babe Ruth
6	1911	Ronald Reagan
6	1923	Zsa Zsa Gabor
7	1812	Charles Dickens
7	1908	Buster Crabbe
8	1819	John Ruskin
8	1828	Jules Verne
8	1920	Lana Turner
8	1925	Jack Lemmon
9	1941	Carole King
9	1946	Mia Farrow
10	1775	Charles Lamb
10	1893	Jimmy Durante
10	1927	Leontyne Price
10	1940	Roberta Flack
11	1847	Thomas Alva Edison
11	1936	Burt Reynolds
12	1809	Charles Darwin
12	1809	Abraham Lincoln
12	1915	Lorne Greene
13	1933	Kim Novak
14	1894	Jack Benny
15	1820	Susan B. Anthony
15	1882	John Barrymore
15	1914	Cesar Romero
16	1838	Henry Adams
16	1904	George F. Kennan
17	1902	Marian Anderson
17	1925	Hal Holbrook
18	1922	Helen Gurley Brown
19	1473	Nicholaus Copernicus
19	1911	Merle Oberon
20	1924	Sidney Poitier
21	1907	W. H. Auden
21	1927	Hubert Givenchy
22	1732	George Washington
22	1810	Frederic Chopin
22	1892	Edna St. Vincent Millay
23	1633	Samuel Pepys
23	1685	George F. Handel
23	1868	William E. B. Du Bois
24	1836	Winslow Homer
25	1841	Pierre Auguste Renoir
25	1873	Enrico Caruso
25	1943	George Harrison
26	1802	Victor Hugo
26	1846	Buffalo Bill Cody
26	1916	Jackie Gleason
26	1924	Tony Randall
26	1928	Fats Domino
26	1932	Johnny Cash
27	1902	John Steinbeck
27	1930	Joanne Woodward
27	1932	Elizabeth Taylor
28	1915	Zero Mostel
28	1939	Tommy Tune

March

1	1910	David Niven
1	1917	Dinah Shore
1	1927	Harry Belafonte
2	1917	Desi Arnaz
3	1847	Alexander Graham Bell

4 1888	Knute Rockne	
5 1908	Rex Harrison	
6 1475	Michelangelo	
6 1806	Elizabeth Barrett Browning	
7 1875	Maurice Ravel	
8 1923	Cyd Charisse	
9 1918	Mickey Spillane	
11 1903	Lawrence Welk	
11 1926	Ralph Abernathy	
12 1948	James Taylor	
13 1910	Sammy Kaye	
14 1879	Albert Einstein	
14 1933	Michael Caine	
15 1767	Andrew Jackson	
16 1751	James Madison	
16 1926	Jerry Lewis	
17 1846	Kate Greenaway	
17 1938	Rudolf Nureyev	
18 1782	John C. Calhoun	
18 1837	Grover Cleveland	
18 1887	Edward Everett Horton	
19 1860	William Jennings Bryan	
19 1938	Ursula Andress	
20 1828	Henrik Ibsen	
20 1907	Ozzie Nelson	
20 1922	Carl Reiner	
20 1931	Hal Linden	
21 1685	Johann Sebastian Bach	
21 1927	Cesar Chavez	
22 1599	Anthony Van Dyck	
22 1891	Chico Marx	
22 1914	Karl Malden	
22 1923	Marcel Marceau	
22 1930	Stephen Sondheim	
23 1908	Joan Crawford	
24 1855	Andrew W. Mellon	

24 1930	Steve McQueen	
25 1867	Arturo Toscanini	
25 1940	Anita Bryant	
25 1942	Aretha Franklin	
25 1947	Elton John	
26 1874	Robert Frost	
26 1911	Tennessee Williams	
26 1931	Leonard Nimoy	
26 1942	Erica Jong	
26 1944	Diana Ross	
27 1886	Mies van der Rohe	
29 1918	Pearl Bailey	
30 1853	Vincent van Gogh	
30 1919	McGeorge Bundy	
30 1937	Warren Beatty	
31 1596	Rene Descartes	
31 1732	Franz Joseph Haydn	

April

1 1815	Otto von Bismarck	
1 1939	Ali MacGraw	
2 1840	Emile Zola	
2 1914	Sir Alec Guinness	
3 1783	Washington Irving	
3 1898	Henry R. Luce	
3 1924	Marlon Brando	
3 1924	Doris Day	
3 1942	Wayne Newton	
5 1856	Booker T. Washington	
5 1900	Spencer Tracy	
5 1908	Bette Davis	
5 1916	Gregory Peck	
6 1874	Harry Houdini	
6 1938	Billy Dee Williams	
7 1770	William Wordsworth	
7 1939	Francis Ford Coppola	
8 1893	Mary Pickford	

8 1912	Sonja Henie
9 1933	Jean-Paul Belmondo
10 1847	Joseph Pulitzer
10 1932	Omar Sharif
10 1934	David Halberstam
11 1913	Oleg Cassini
12 1777	Henry Clay
12 1919	Ann Miller
13 1743	Thomas Jefferson
13 1906	Samuel Beckett
14 1932	Loretta Lynn
15 1843	Henry James
16 1867	Wilbur Wright
16 1889	Charlie Chaplin
16 1921	Peter Ustinov
17 1894	Nikita Khrushchev
17 1918	William Holden
18 1938	Charley Pride
19 1933	Jayne Mansfield
19 1935	Dudley Moore
20 1808	Napoleon III
20 1889	Adolph Hitler
20 1893	Harold Lloyd
20 1949	Jessica Lange
21 1816	Charlotte Bronte
21 1916	Anthony Quinn
21 1926	Queen Elizabeth II
22 1904	J. Robert Oppenheimer
22 1908	Eddie Albert
22 1937	Jack Nicholson
23 1813	Stephen A. Douglas
23 1928	Shirley Temple Black
24 1856	Henri Philippe Petain
24 1934	Shirley MacLaine
24 1942	Barbra Streisand
25 1599	Oliver Cromwell
25 1874	Guglielmo Marconi
25 1918	Ella Fitzgerald

25 1940	Al Pacino
26 1936	Carol Burnett
27 1791	Samuel F. B. Morse
27 1822	Ulysses S. Grant
27 1934	Anouk Aimee
28 1758	James Monroe
28 1878	Lionel Barrymore
28 1941	Ann-Margret
29 1919	Celeste Holm
30 1912	Eve Arden

May

1 1909	Kate Smith
1 1918	Jack Paar
1 1939	Judy Collins
2 1729	Catherine the Great
2 1904	Bing Crosby
2 1924	Theodore Bikel
2 1935	King Hussein
3 1849	Jacob A. Riis
3 1934	James Brown
4 1796	Horace Mann
4 1929	Audrey Hepburn
5 1818	Karl Marx
5 1914	Tyrone Power
6 1758	Robespierre
6 1856	Sigmund Freud
6 1895	Rudolph Valentino
6 1915	Orson Welles
7 1812	Robert Browning
7 1833	Johannes Brahms
7 1840	Tchaikovsky
7 1901	Gary Cooper
7 1923	Anne Baxter
8 1884	Harry S. Truman
8 1940	Ricky Nelson
9 1800	John Brown

9 1936	Albert Finney	
9 1936	Glenda Jackson	
9 1946	Candice Bergen	
10 1899	Fred Astaire	
11 1888	Irving Berlin	
11 1904	Salvador Dali	
12 1820	Florence Nightingale	
13 1907	Daphne Du Maurier	
13 1914	Joe Louis	
14 1936	Bobby Darin	
15 1950	Stevie Wonder	
16 1905	Henry Fonda	
16 1919	Liberace	
17 1955	Sugar Ray Leonard	
18 1897	Frank Capra	
18 1919	Dame Margot Fonteyn	
18 1945	Reggie Jackson	
19 1795	Johns Hopkins	
20 1799	Honore de Balzac	
20 1908	James Stewart	
20 1946	Cher	
21 1917	Raymond Burr	
22 1859	Sir Arthur Conan Doyle	
22 1907	Sir Laurence Olivier	
23 1883	Douglas Fairbanks	
23 1928	Rosemary Clooney	
24 1819	Queen Victoria	
24 1941	Bob Dylan	
25 1803	Ralph Waldo Emerson	
25 1926	Miles Davis	
26 1886	Al Jolson	
26 1907	John Wayne	
27 1878	Isadora Duncan	
27 1912	John Cheever	
28 1944	Gladys Knight	
29 1903	Bob Hope	
29 1917	John F. Kennedy	
30 1909	Benny Goodman	

31 1819	Walt Whitman	
31 1908	Don Ameche	
31 1931	Clint Eastwood	

June

1 1801	Brigham Young	
1 1926	Marilyn Monroe	
1 1934	Pat Boone	
2 1840	Thomas Hardy	
2 1904	Johnny Weissmuller	
3 1808	Jefferson Davis	
3 1925	Tony Curtis	
3 1926	Alan Ginsberg	
4 1908	Rosalind Russell	
6 1755	Nathan Hale	
6 1875	Thomas Mann	
7 1909	Jessica Tandy	
7 1940	Tom Jones	
8 1869	Frank Lloyd Wright	
9 1672	Peter the Great	
9 1893	Cole Porter	
10 1904	Frederick Loewe	
10 1922	Judy Garland	
11 1864	Richard Strauss	
11 1910	Jacques Cousteau	
13 1865	William Butler Yeats	
13 1892	Basil Rathbone	
14 1811	Harriet Beecher Stowe	
14 1909	Burl Ives	
15 1902	Erik Erikson	
16 1890	Stan Laurel	
16 1937	Erich Segal	
17 1914	John Hersey	
17 1917	Dean Martin	
18 1896	Philip Barry	
18 1942	Paul McCartney	
19 1902	Guy Lombardo	

45

19 1903	Lou Gehrig	
20 1905	Lillian Hellman	
20 1924	Audie Murphy	
21 1882	Rockwell Kent	
21 1922	Judy Holliday	
22 1906	Billy Wilder	
22 1921	Joseph Papp	
22 1922	Bill Blass	
23 1927	Bob Fosse	
24 1895	Jack Dempsey	
25 1945	Carly Simon	
26 1892	Pearl Buck	
26 1904	Peter Lorre	
27 1880	Helen Keller	
28 1902	Richard Rodgers	
28 1867	Luigi Pirandello	
29 1901	Nelson Eddy	
30 1917	Lena Horne	

July

1 1916	Olivia De Havilland
1 1931	Leslie Caron
1 1961	Princess Diana
4 1804	Nathaniel Hawthorne
4 1900	Louis Armstrong
4 1927	Neil Simon
5 1804	George Sand
5 1810	P. T. Barnum
5 1909	Andre Gromyko
6 1747	John Paul Jones
6 1925	Merv Griffin
7 1899	George Cukor
7 1922	Pierre Cardin
9 1819	Elias Howe
10 1509	John Calvin
10 1871	Marcel Proust
10 1915	Saul Bellow

10 1920	David Brinkley
10 1947	Arlo Guthrie
11 1767	John Quincy Adams
11 1920	Yul Brynner
12 1817	Henry David Thoreau
12 1895	Oscar Hammerstein II
12 1895	Buckminster Fuller
12 1908	Milton Berle
12 1937	Bill Cosby
14 1918	Ingmar Bergman
15 1573	Inigo Jones
15 1606	Rembrandt
16 1821	Mary Baker Eddy
16 1907	Barbara Stanwyck
16 1911	Ginger Rogers
17 1763	John Jacob Astor
17 1900	James Cagney
17 1931	Diahann Carroll
18 1913	Red Skelton
18 1921	John H. Glenn, Jr.
19 1834	Edgar Degas
20 1919	Sir Edmund Hillary
20 1938	Natalie Wood
21 1899	Ernest Hemingway
21 1920	Isaac Stern
21 1952	Robin Williams
22 1890	Rose Kennedy
22 1898	Stephen Vincent Benet
22 1932	Oscar De La Renta
24 1783	Simon Bolivar
24 1898	Amelia Earhart
26 1856	George Bernard Shaw
26 1922	Blake Edwards
26 1928	Stanley Kubrick
26 1944	Mick Jagger
28 1901	Rudy Vallee
29 1883	Benito Mussolini
30 1863	Henry Ford
30 1941	Paul Anka

August

1	1819	Herman Melville
2	1905	Myrna Loy
2	1924	James Baldwin
2	1924	Carroll O'Connor
2	1933	Peter O'Toole
3	1900	Ernie Pyle
3	1940	Martin Sheen
4	1792	Percy Bysshe Shelley
5	1850	Guy de Maupassant
5	1906	John Huston
5	1930	Neil Armstrong
6	1809	Alfred, Lord Tennyson
6	1911	Lucille Ball
6	1917	Robert Mitchum
8	1923	Esther Williams
8	1937	Dustin Hoffman
10	1874	Herbert Hoover
10	1928	Jimmy Dean
11	1925	Mike Douglas
12	1881	Cecil B. De Mille
13	1899	Alfred Hitchcock
13	1926	Fidel Castro
14	1930	Earl Weaver
15	1769	Napoleon Bonaparte
15	1771	Sir Walter Scott
15	1887	Edna Ferber
15	1912	Julia Child
17	1892	Mae West
17	1943	Robert De Niro
18	1937	Robert Redford
19	1871	Orville Wright
19	1893	Alfred Lunt
19	1902	Ogden Nash
19	1919	Malcolm Forbes
20	1818	Emily Bronte
21	1904	Count Basie
22	1862	Claude Debussy
22	1920	Ray Bradbury
22	1940	Valerie Harper
23	1912	Gene Kelly
25	1530	Ivan the Terrible
25	1909	Ruby Keeler
25	1918	Leonard Bernstein
25	1930	Sean Connery
27	1871	Theodore Dreiser
27	1908	Lyndon B. Johnson
28	1899	Charles Boyer
28	1925	Donald O'Connor
29	1916	Ingrid Bergman
29	1923	Richard Attenborough
31	1908	William Saroyan
31	1918	Alan Jay Lerner
31	1924	Buddy Hackett
31	1928	James Coburn

September

3	1913	Alan Ladd
4	1917	Henry Ford II
4	1931	Mitzi Gaynor
5	1902	Darryl F. Zanuck
5	1929	Bob Newhart
5	1940	Raquel Welch
6	1860	Jane Addams
7	1533	Queen Elizabeth I
7	1909	Elia Kazan
7	1923	Peter Lawford
8	1157	Richard the Lionhearted
8	1889	Robert A. Taft
8	1922	Sid Caesar
8	1925	Peter Sellers
11	1862	O. Henry
12	1888	Maurice Chevalier

47

12 1913	Jesse Owens	
13 1905	Claudette Colbert	
13 1925	Mel Torme	
13 1944	Jacqueline Bisset	
15 1789	James Fenimore Cooper	
15 1857	William Howard Taft	
15 1922	Jackie Cooper	
16 1924	Lauren Bacall	
16 1925	B. B. King	
17 1931	Anne Bancroft	
18 1905	Greta Garbo	
20 1878	Upton Sinclair	
20 1934	Sophia Loren	
21 1866	H. G. Wells	
22 1902	John Houseman	
23 1920	Mickey Rooney	
23 1932	Ray Charles	
25 1844	Sarah Bernhardt	
25 1931	Barbara Walters	
26 1888	T. S. Eliot	
26 1898	George Gershwin	
26 1948	Olivia Newton-John	
27 1722	Samuel Adams	
28 1909	Al Capp	
28 1924	Marcello Mastroianni	
29 1901	Enrico Fermi	
29 1907	Gene Autry	
29 1908	Greer Garson	
29 1935	Jerry Lee Lewis	
30 1921	Deborah Kerr	
30 1921	Truman Capote	
30 1935	Johnny Mathis	

October

1 1904	Vladimir Horowitz
1 1920	Walter Matthau
2 1452	King Richard III

2 1869	Mohandas Gandhi
2 1895	Groucho Marx
2 1904	Graham Greene
3 1900	Thomas Wolfe
3 1925	Gore Vidal
4 1924	Charlton Heston
6 1820	Jenny Lind
6 1887	Le Corbusier
6 1909	Carole Lombard
7 1923	June Allyson
8 1941	Jesse Jackson
9 1940	John Lennon
10 1813	Giuseppe Verdi
10 1900	Helen Hayes
10 1930	Harold Pinter
10 1946	Ben Vereen
11 1884	Eleanor Roosevelt
11 1916	Jerome Robbins
14 1644	William Penn
14 1890	Dwight D. Eisenhower
14 1927	Roger Moore
15 1844	Friedrich W. Nietzsche
15 1908	John Kenneth Galbraith
16 1888	Eugene O'Neill
16 1925	Angela Lansbury
16 1927	Gunter Grass
17 1915	Arthur Miller
17 1928	Rita Hayworth
17 1930	Jimmy Breslin
18 1927	George C. Scott
20 1632	Sir Christopher Wren
20 1911	Will Rogers, Jr.
20 1925	Art Buchwald
21 1772	Samuel Coleridge
21 1833	Alfred Nobel
22 1811	Franz Liszt
22 1943	Catherine Deneuve
23 1925	Johnny Carson
25 1838	Georges Bizet

25 1881	Pablo Picasso
25 1941	Helen Reddy
26 1935	Rich Little
27 1858	Theodore Roosevelt
28 1914	Jonas Salk
29 1740	James Boswell
29 1947	Richard Dreyfuss
30 1735	John Adams
31 1887	Chiang Kai-shek
31 1936	Michael Landon

November

2 1755	Marie Antoinette
2 1913	Burt Lancaster
3 1922	Charles Bronson
4 1879	Will Rogers
4 1916	Walter Cronkite
4 1918	Art Carney
5 1912	Roy Rogers
5 1913	Vivien Leigh
6 1854	John Philip Sousa
6 1931	Mike Nichols
6 1946	Sally Field
7 1867	Marie Curie
7 1918	Billy Graham
7 1926	Joan Sutherland
7 1943	Joni Mitchell
8 1909	Katharine Hepburn
9 1841	King Edward VII
9 1915	Hedy Lamarr
10 1483	Martin Luther
10 1890	Claude Rains
10 1925	Richard Burton
11 1821	Fedor M. Dostoevski
11 1925	Jonathan Winters
12 1929	Grace Kelly
13 1850	Robert Louis Stevenson

14 1840	Claude Monet
14 1889	Jawaharlal Nehru
14 1900	Aaron Copland
14 1912	Barbara Hutton
14 1919	Veronica Lake
14 1948	Prince Charles
15 1934	Petula Clark
15 1940	Sam Waterston
16 1908	Burgess Meredith
17 1925	Rock Hudson
18 1901	George Gallup
18 1909	Johnny Mercer
18 1923	Alan B. Shepard, Jr.
19 1752	George Rogers Clark
19 1831	James A. Garfield
19 1917	Indira Gandhi
19 1936	Dick Cavett
20 1908	Alistair Cooke
20 1920	Gene Tierney
20 1939	Dick Smothers
21 1694	Voltaire
21 1943	Marlo Thomas
21 1945	Goldie Hawn
22 1819	George Eliot
22 1869	Andre Gide
22 1890	Charles de Gaulle
22 1899	Hoagy Carmichael
22 1924	Geraldine Page
23 1893	Harpo Marx
24 1914	Geraldine Fitzgerald
24 1925	William F. Buckley
25 1835	Andrew Carnegie
26 1922	Charles Schulz
28 1757	William Blake
29 1832	Louisa May Alcott
30 1667	Jonathan Swift
30 1835	Mark Twain
30 1874	Winston Churchill
30 1929	Dick Clark

December

1 1914	Mary Martin
1 1935	Woody Allen
2 1924	Alexander Haig
2 1925	Julie Harris
3 1930	Jean-Luc Godard
4 1892	Francisco Franco
5 1901	Walt Disney
6 1857	Joseph Conrad
6 1896	Ira Gershwin
6 1920	Dave Brubeck
7 1875	Willa Cather
7 1932	Ellen Burstyn
8 1765	Eli Whitney
8 1925	Sammy Davis, Jr.
8 1933	Flip Wilson
9 1608	John Milton
9 1909	Douglas Fairbanks, Jr.
9 1916	Kirk Douglas
9 1922	Redd Foxx
9 1929	John Cassavetes
9 1941	Beau Bridges
10 1830	Emily Dickinson
10 1914	Dorothy Lamour
11 1931	Rita Moreno
12 1821	Gustave Flaubert
12 1893	Edward G. Robinson
12 1915	Frank Sinatra
13 1835	Phillips Brooks
13 1925	Dick Van Dyke
13 1929	Christopher Plummer
14 1895	King George VI
14 1946	Patty Duke
15 37	Nero
15 1892	J. Paul Getty
16 1775	Jane Austen
16 1899	Noel Coward
16 1939	Liv Ullmann
18 1886	Ty Cobb
18 1916	Betty Grable
19 1902	Sir Ralph Richardson
19 1906	Leonid Brezhnev
19 1939	Cicely Tyson
20 1904	Irene Dunne
21 1804	Benjamin Disraeli
21 1879	Joseph Stalin
21 1937	Jane Fonda
22 1858	Giacomo Puccini
24 1905	Howard Hughes
24 1922	Ava Gardner
24 1930	Robert Joffrey
25 1642	Isaac Newton
25 1821	Clara Barton
25 1899	Humphrey Bogart
25 1907	Cab Calloway
25 1924	Rod Serling
26 1914	Richard Widmark
26 1927	Alan King
27 1822	Louis Pasteur
27 1901	Marlene Dietrich
28 1856	Woodrow Wilson
29 1808	Andrew Johnson
29 1937	Mary Tyler Moore
29 1938	Jon Voight
30 1865	Rudyard Kipling
30 1914	Bert Parks
31 1869	Henri Matisse
31 1943	John Denver

PERSONAL

Birthday

Register

AUGUST